D A I S Y,

My Life As A Joy Guide

By Daisy

Channeled by
Dale Epley

Copyright © 2009 Dale Epley
All rights reserved.
Printed in the United States of America.

ISBN: 0-9773474-0-0
ISBN-13: 9780977347407

For additional copies of this book,
any of the meditation CDs or tapes,
please contact Dale Epley at 1-800-421-0505.

See additional information on the meditations available in back of book.

My Life As A Joy Guide

This book has been written to help each person understand just one possible small portion of his/her own spiritual journey. We have tried to give you a glimpse into the interaction between Daisy and Dale… Joy Guide and human. In doing so, we hope that it is entertaining, as well as educational.

The possibilities are unlimited. Learning to work with, and trust your own teachers and spirit guides is a major step forward. You will have ample opportunity to compare your own journey as you read Daisy's words.

Learn to interact with spirit not only with serious and devoted intent, but also with fun and games. Keep a light heart, and with that light heart you are allowing light to guide your way.

The most important thing to remember as you read this book is to keep an open mind and to realize that the mystery of the unseen world of spirit is just another dimension.

Dale Epley

❦

Acknowledgements

From Dale

To my husband, Jerry… thanks for your love and patience as I disappeared   for long periods of time to work in this special world of spirit.

Thanks goes to the many dear friends that answered my call for help in trying to figure out the format for this book. Sharra McDearmont of Round Rock, Texas, was especially patient and creative in her quick response to my call for help, and I owe a debt of gratitude to her for her 'extra mile'.

I also wish to thank another long time friend, Russ McCaw of Louisville, Kentucky, for his advice and encouragement when I first set out to create this book with Daisy.

And to Daisy, thank you for your patience with me as we worked together. It's been fun and informative for me, and probably quite exasperating for you trying to get me to focus on this project.

Lily, one of my teachers in spirit, is the inspiration for Daisy, and for me. We are both grateful to her for her love and generosity of spirit in sharing with us.

To all of my Angels, teachers and guides in Spirit… I want to thank each of you for the support, patience, and guidance received from each of you. Without you, this book would never have been finished.

Contents

Introduction

(Dale)

It was late one afternoon, December of 1970… seems like only a few days ago, but there I was, in a huge funk… and no one to talk to.

Actually, I didn't realize it at that time, but I had lots of people to talk to. It took me about twenty more years to recognize them and to begin interaction with them. The people I speak of are those in Spirit already. There are my loved ones that have passed on, but there are also those that are here to keep me company… to guide me (when I allow), to balance my energy, and to teach me (when I allow). The people I deal mostly with today in Spirit (my Angels, Teachers, Guides, Fairies, and Divas) were only a whisper, a thought, or even a dream back in those early days.

For some time, even from my childhood, I had been able to just stare into space, or at an object, or even a person (but that could be embarrassing). I could just disappear in my mind. My spirit teachers tell me I was hiding; that I had discovered a safe place inside self.

I don't think I had an abusive childhood at all, but there was much sadness because my Mom was our only support and was always busy. My sister was six years older than I; she just didn't have time for a kid sister always hanging around her. But I do know there was love… just not enough time to indulge in a lot of it.

As a child, my main activity was the energy I created with my mind. I interacted with inanimate things and could pretend they were real. I loved the little plastic or glass horses and dogs, and spent a lot of time creating a farm or house outlined with small rocks for the driveway, the corrals, and all sorts of things that I imagined.

I began to 'hide' as I grew older and recognized my inferiority to other people. I was, and am, as smart as anyone, but had little desire for school. Sitting still for long periods of time was a real bore, and those were the times I really began to exercise my ability to disappear. Of course, it proved embarrassing when a teacher would call on me, and I had no idea of the subject being talked about.

Funny thing, though, I've always been hungry to learn. As I grew older, and entered the everyday work world, I often took evening classes on one subject or another. I eventually realized that my life and interests had changed. I recognized my journey as a psychic/medium, and as such… I became a full time student of Metaphysics.

When I first began to open to Spirit, it was truly a wild ride… but **that** will be another book. This one is about one of my teachers. Her name is Daisy, and she is my Joy Guide. This book is by and about Daisy, written by Daisy through me… one of her channels.

And, so we begin…

*This Impression of Daisy was created by Sharon Beth Wilder
Of Fisherville, KY. See more of her artwork, including tarot deck
and book, prints, and key chains at www.twilightrealm.us*

Chapter 1

Play Time

I am Daisy, a Joy Guide, and I really **love** that exalted title, but truly... I'm more than what my title implies!

As a Joy Guide, in this particular lifetime with Dale, I have many and varied duties, but they are **all** fun for me, and I try to make them fun for her, too. The one I cherish the most, is telling her what to do! Well, truthfully... I don't really do that... she's a stubborn person, and wouldn't really be agreeable to me telling her what to do. But I do give her ideas... like writing this book.

A really great artist (and friend) who works with Spirit in much the same way as Dale, did my portrait recently. His name is John Duckett, and I must say that he did an excellent job. (I am sad to say that his was a pencil drawing and we could not get it to print dark enough for this book.) The idea for this book kind of grew from John's portrait of me, Dale's desire to create a book, and my ambition to be better known by all of you. But, not just me... I want all of you to know your own Joy Guide, and to understand that we **are** a reality and can be very useful to you and for you.

You see, we in the spirit world who are called Joy Guides are from many different walks of life. I happen to be a 'Sprite' or 'Fairy'... and I love to create happiness. There are also Angels, Elves, Cherubs, Divas, and even some human souls that are Joy Guides... we are quite varied, aren't we?

Let's get back to my stubborn human and my efforts to keep her in line. She does have a mind of her own, and free will, and definitely uses it. But, the real magic happens when she goes into quiet time and connects with those of us on this side of the veil to find guidance.

We can't fool her for long. If the information does not feel right or sound right, she goes even deeper to her truth... the part of her that touches God.

Joy Guides typically appear as youngsters - from four to nine years old… though we can actually create the illusion of ANY age we desire (but kids get away with a lot more than an adult would). Dale sometimes calls me incorrigible, but it's all good innocent, fun. When I do something that upsets her, I try never to do that kind of thing again.

We love the vibration of singing and dancing, and the things that make you feel good give us extra energy, too. For instance, I often move things around (little things that are easily moved like keys, coins, etc.) I did lots of that through the years, but it hardly got noticed, because Dale just thought she had misplaced things.

Recently, she's beginning to notice these things more. Last year, we attended a workshop where some people were talking about the higher vibrations helping Spirit to create more play. Dale was a bit upset because she felt she was missing out since nothing was happening like that in her life. HA! If she only knew!!

Anyway, I decided to up the energy a bit and create so she would know we could do similar things. One of the first things was the shower… she thought **she** kept forgetting to change the water flow from the showerhead to the lower faucet. When she would turn the water on, the shower would start and get her all wet. HA! **That** was great fun… and pretty innocent.

She soon figured it out so the surprise was gone (except for every once in awhile I'll do it just to keep her on her toes). Actually, she double-checks most of the time now to make sure the shower is off.

The best ever was with the little measuring spoon in the coffee. I just helped it to disappear. Coffee is a daily routine, and there was no place else the spoon could be. It was always right on top of the coffee waiting to prepare another pot. Well, she searched and searched, but couldn't find it. A day or two later, when I remembered my responsibility, I made it reappear back in the coffee can.

These things are irritating, I know… but they also represent that we are real, and **that** is exciting to Dale. She loves when we surprise her with a light turned on that was off or vise-verse. Only one time have I been truly sorry, though. Dale's husband, Jerry, was putting new carpet in our office, and had to disconnect all of the computer stuff. Well, he didn't like the mouse that was being used, so he decided to buy another one. I really loved that mouse; all shiny black with a big red ball that lit up in the center. Well, he **said** he was going to get another one, and I liked that one so well that I was able to pull it to **my** side of the veil... oh, it was wonderful. A **great** toy, but it took lots of energy to get it.

The problem was that I took it too soon. They looked and looked all over for a day or two and couldn't find it. Dale felt bad because she knew I had it and Jerry was getting upset about the disappearance. I felt bad because Dale said for me to keep it if I liked it so much. I knew better, and really tried to give it back to them. I found I was too scattered to do it.

So, guess what! I asked for help. We encourage all of you to ask for help, so I figured I could, too. And I got it! Damien (my friend, and Dale's guardian angel) helped me create the energy to give it back. We put it way up high on top of a shelf, so they would think they might have done it! Dale said I could have it back, but it was too nerve-wracking... NO, THANK YOU!

Not all of us Joy Guides play tricks, but guess it's just my nature to do so. I try to encourage all the other Joy Guides to learn these games to add excitement to their lives and their human's life... but many are too afraid or too shy.

We **all** love to be recognized by you, so just ask either in your mind or out loud, "What's my Joy Guide's name?" and listen quietly, you'll either hear a name or it will be in your thoughts... REALLY! If all else fails, ask Dale... she'll tell you!

Chapter 2

The Beginning

In the beginning of time, God created all that stuff you read about, and already know about... so we won't go too deeply there... just the area that concerns ME!

Well, I didn't exist at that time, anyway... but did come along into reality at about the time Noah brought all the animals together during the flood. God decided that the earth plane needed some major help to regenerate, so he created me... and hundreds of others like me to get busy.

In an effort to help earth to truly flower again, we helped to sow the seeds and seedlings from our world to yours. We did a truly beautiful job, and even though many of the original species do not exist anymore... new ones took their place, and the earth is still a beautiful flower garden in many places, large and small. As the earth began to be populated again, I decided I wanted to branch out more and work with people, instead of tending the flowers and trees. So, I asked God to help me find just the right kind of work, and **this** it.

I was with Dale right in the beginning, and not only while she was on the earth plane in any of her lives, but with her on other planetary systems, and while she was in spirit, too. I feel mine is a very important job, because the interaction with the human world is something that is necessary and good.

The way she and I met was in the spirit world (I must explain that 'she' has not always been a 'she' in all her lifetimes, but we'll stick with her name of today to keep from confusion). We actually did what you would call an interview with each other, and found we were very compatible.

My original duties, while in the spirit world, were to teach her about the pitfalls as well as the positive things about each of the worlds she would visit... but, I must admit, I was not the only one there to do this. While a human soul is truly in spirit, and not on the earth plane, there are many things to keep them busy. Dale's mission was to learn more about the healing arts in all its forms. Of course, she uses only about a tenth of these abilities now, but can go deeper into her knowledge if she desires to, and works to release the doubts surrounding her abilities.

When I am allowed to create the things that I need to create to do my work, I find great satisfaction. Dale is the person who does not allow me to do all I can to help, but it is not at all a bad thing that she doesn't. She's very independent, and wants to do as much as she can to learn to create for herself. What I'm saying is... each of you has a joy guide just like me, and each of us can make life so much easier for you if you would allow us to. But it is not on the conscious level that you make these decisions. We hold meetings on the Astral Plain from time to time and your soul makes these decisions.

When we first came together, as I said, we were very compatible... but did not often work on the conscious level as we do now. It's taken a few centuries for us to evolve together in our work and relationship to this point. This is the first lifetime that I have been recognized by Dale on the conscious level as a teacher/irritant in her life.

But I've always been here, doing what I could to help her along. The way I've worked with her in the past was in decision making. When she was younger and did not recognize me in her life, sometimes she would get really sad and depressed... she could 'talk' herself into a happier place. Ha! That was ME!! She just thought SHE was talking to herself... helping herself to get out of that negative space.

Other times, we would have discussions about the beautiful things we could notice, or work on a difficult situation at home or work. I do admit.... my voice was not the only one... there are many Angels and guides that are available to each of you for this task.

The most important thing for you to realize is that you are not alone in your world. And I'm not alone, either... there are many people here in my world that love you and are there with you because you are special. We have a desire to see you succeed in all areas of your life.

Chapter 3

Conscious Awareness

As we began to build our relationship in this lifetime, Dale and I had one truly common thread to link us to our truth... that one thread was to break all barriers to the successful culmination of our work together.

Now, to break **all** barriers might be a little high in expectation... but we do feel that we have come a long way. The really neat thing is that as we create new (and old) stuff for Dale to experience and to learn... she, in turn, shares the information with others. We do this in workshops, lectures, meditations, and in the private readings that she does for people.

She learns from her clients and students, too, of course. They often ask questions that she doesn't know the answer to... that's when Spirit can truly teach. Sometimes she does get in the way, especially if there's a subject that she has learned really well. She has learned to recognize when this happens, and to ask us if the information is from Spirit or herself.

That's the idea of learning to work with us. In opening up your own psychic abilities, you will find that the more you work with us, the better your skills become. Some of you will excel quickly to a place where you are quite comfortable, and others will proceed more slowly. Each of you is unique, and each of you will grow into the spiritual person that is your soul if you will only open up and try.

The fears that will hold some of you back are there because you created this lifetime to work on these particular issues. So, if you truly desire to progress quickly, learn to heal those things you are afraid of. There are **so** many ways to do this. Dale has taught her ways of healing to many, and we even have guided meditations on tape and CD just for this type of thing because we feel it is so important. But you must find what is right for **you**, and to do this, you must experiment with many different techniques.

7

Workshops, classes, and trying out the different techniques that are taught through various books are just a few examples of how to find the right stuff for you. Read all you can about how others have opened to their spiritual awareness. Read with your heart and mind open, slow down and study when necessary. If you find information that does not seem right to you, release it, and continue to read.

Discuss the information you learn with others... the things you believe **and** the things that you do not. You could even create a monthly discussion group focusing on one book at a time.

Any time you read anything that gives directions or examples... try it... you might be surprised at what happens! And right here, I will tell you that any book channeled by any of us in the Spirit world... the spirit that wrote the book is actually available to you, so...TALK to me!! Here I am! Just call my name a couple of times, and I'll visit with you.

Chapter 4
How To Contact Your Guides

The most important thing to remember is... one more time, now... each of you is unique and each of you will open to our world in your own way and in your own time. Each of you will work with your own people in spirit, also in your own way. Other people, books, and workshops will always be very helpful in guiding you, but don't be disappointed if something doesn't work the same for you as it does for another.

It would be very handy if you would record the following, so you can just relax and hear your own voice giving you these directions.

Thank you, God, for your love and protection.

Begin by just relaxing.... take a big, deep breath and release. Again, breathe deeply through the nose, bring the air all the way down into the tummy area, and release slowly through the mouth. One more time, now... breathe deeply through the nose, and as you release this time feel all the tension release with it.

Just sit quietly for a moment and feel the peace all around you. Now, ask your Joy Guide to come forward to meet with you at a special place. In your mind, see a beautiful brook.... the sun is shining on it, and there is a trail beside the brook with flowers all around the trail.

Begin to walk on the trail... it will take you to a special place... YOU create the place! (It might be a small clearing in the forest, or a place beside the little brook, or maybe the brook joins the ocean, and you create a space there on the beach. The trail may even lead you to a small house or cabin... it doesn't matter... this is your own special, private, safe place.)

Enter this special place you've created... find a comfortable place and relax. Now, you might get to this special place first.... so just wait a bit.... but if you will make an effort to meet your Joy Guide there often... I'll just bet he/she might get there before you!

Some of you will see a person, some will see a light, or vapor... some will not see anything. Others will hear, or communicate in some other way. Some will be able to feel the energy of the guide. Anything goes, we ask you to just be open and aware.

Now, if you have problems and do not see, feel, or hear anything... don't worry... you are normal! It takes practice to open up any of these avenues into our world. Please don't give up, just keep trying... I know you'll get there!

Instead of the journey, you might just get yourself relaxed with the breathing technique, quiet the mind, and just ask for the name of your Joy Guide. If you think of a name at that moment.... use it to connect with her/him.

The major problem we have with all of you is that you disbelieve. You might see us out of the corner of your eye... you say it was your imagination! You might hear us talking to you... you say it was your imagination! You might feel a light touch... you say it was your imagination!

Now, most of the teachers here are very patient... not me!! I want to get on with this stuff. If you don't try or you keep denying the little gifts we try to give you to recognize us... I can really get irritated... But, that's ok, that's life, and I get over it in about two of your minutes!

There are lots of ways we can talk with you. If you can't hear us, then work with a pendulum, we also can manipulate tarot cards, runes, I Ching...there are **so** many ways to work with us. But if you want to talk to just your Joy Guide.... please specify... just say so!

Often, during our private readings, a guide, teacher, or angel will introduce him/herself to our client. This is always really exciting, especially when the client can perceive their presence in some way. The following is sent to us from **Kim Sheffield** of Louisville, Kentucky about a reading with Dale.

It was from my first reading with you in March of 2004. You were telling me about one of my guides. You said his name was Patrick O... then you said, no, it's Patricko. (I've got this on tape and listened to it more than once over the years). You said he was right in front of me and asked me if I could see him.

I said I sensed someone big and tall with broad shoulders, I got the sense he was an Indian (which struck me odd, because Patricko sounded Spanish or Italian). You said he wanted to give me a hug, so I "hugged" him. I felt that he was big and strong, yet gentle. I felt protected.

Now, during the reading, you said that I'd meet my mate in either 2 months or 2 years, we both had stuff to take care of and it was our choice. Two months later, May 6, 2004, Patrick Owens called me out of the blue - hadn't spoken to him in over 21 years.

He said he had thought of me often over the years, and when he did he said a prayer that I was always okay. He said that for the past two weeks he had thought of me and prayed, but he couldn't get me out of his mind and he was worried. (I had been in tears and prayer much of those two weeks, worried about continuing Nursing School full time and finances in keeping my home.)

Patrick said he had searched for me in the past years without success, but this time found me. I emailed you, Dale, to ask you if it was possible that Patricko was my to-be husband or was he definitely my guide. You told me he was my guide. I asked you again more recently if that guide was still around and you told me that no, he was no longer needed.

It gave me comfort that my guide's name was Patricko (made me think Patrick Owens) and I had been talking to Patricko ever since you gave me his name. I think my guide came to me this way to open me to trusting the relationship. It REALLY made a big difference in my comfort level in moving forward in my relationship with Pat.

My Pat, by the way, is Irish . . . and over 50% American Indian, 6'5", big and broad shouldered. We're married and he's even more wonderful as a husband than I imagined possible. I'm very spoiled.

Yes, I **treasure** *that meeting with my guide and my hug.*

Chapter 5

Pitfalls, Hazards, Uncertainties

There could be a whole book written about this one.... but it's necessary to help you understand a few things about opening up to our world.

First of all, you must realize your own belief system is at work. This includes your deep 'knowing' and all the fears and taboos that are associated with experiencing spiritual growth. Many of you have been taught you will attract 'demons' or negative spirits who are just waiting to get to you. Most of you have experienced reading a book or watching a movie about the horrible things that can happen if you try to enter into the Spirit world. I will tell you this... truly there is nothing but love that we work with.

Yes, of course, there are negative factors that exist in the Universe... just as there are negative factors to be faced in your earth reality. But, I say to you, each of you is well guarded by those people in spirit that love you, and you cannot be harmed unless you, yourself, open up to the possibility.

Prayer, trust, faith... all of these are a part of our reality, and when you work with these same tools in dealing with our world.... how can you possibly fail to be safe??

Demons? Where? There are none here, though you might hear of their existence even from some of your psychics, healers, etc. on the earth plane. They only exist in your mind, and your mind is **powerful**... if they exist in your mind, they can certainly become a reality physically.

YOU are human on the earth plane.... but, you are above all...Soul.... and you have existed for a number of centuries (earth time). You probably have experienced many other lifetimes on the earth plane, and possibly in other planetary systems. In these other lifetimes, there have been many positive and negative experiences. The positive ones, we don't need to be concerned with, but the negative ones are the ones we often see playing havoc with you.

You bring many of these experiences into this lifetime in cell memory. Most are there because you desired to work at healing them during this incarnation. And these can create all kinds of problems for those of you who are not yet certain about what's happening. For instance... you may have been murdered in another life, and depending on how you were put to death, you may deal with the present day cell memory in many different ways. One is to create the pain of that death in today's reality.

Let me explain more fully... if, for instance, someone put a knife through your heart. That death could possible create a similar pain around the heart in this life, and it might happen at about the same age as you were when you experienced it in that other life. It could also create one or more ailments concerning the heart.

You may have drowned in the ocean, or been eaten by a large fish, or died adrift in the seemingly endless ocean at some time in the past. Consequently, you may have an unexplained fear about the ocean in this life.

The same can be said about fear of fire, animals, people with certain characteristics, and any number of fears in this life. If there is no logical explanation for the fear in this life, you can bet it's probably based on the past.

There are many ways to heal these past life memories... books to deal with them, healers to help you deal with them, meditations, etc. But the main thing is to deal with them! Face those fears and learn to heal them, so you can move forward unimpeded. You will find a number of guided meditations available on CD or cassette tape listed in the back of this book to help you deal with fears. These fears can actually be barriers to your own psychic or healing abilities and to your good health.

Childhood experiences can also create fears to be dealt with. Any time you experience any memory from your childhood that creates pain for you in any way... that pain represents the child you were, calling out for help. Stop what you are doing if at all possible, and see that child in your mind. Imagine holding that younger you in your arms lovingly, and ask God to help that child grow into the adult you, so that both of you may strengthen and heal.

Learning to trust is a most magical journey. Learning to know what is you and what is guidance from those of us in Spirit is very important. We (your teachers, guides, angels, loved ones) will **never** do anything to harm you, will never give orders to you at all. Always look at the information carefully if you are uncertain about it; never do anything that would cause you harm or harm to anyone else. Always use common sense about the information you get from what you consider to be the Spirit world.

What you must realize is that each of you is multi-faceted... multi-personalitied, and control is a very large part of your existence on the earth plane. Especially in the beginning of your journey, information can come from a part of yourself that might hurt or embarrass you or another in some way.

Again, if the information received does not feel right or sound right, wrap it in love and release it to the Universe. Always ask for God's intervention and guidance. It may not come in an obvious way, but it WILL come.

This art was created by Eva M. Sakmar-Sullivan
Of Mars, PA. www.stardolphin.com

Chapter 6

The Angels & Me

Too many times, I have had doubts about my abilities to help those of you on the earth plain to the extent truly needed. It is especially hard to realize you sometimes do not even wish to have help. But I don't give up; I try never to be dissuaded in my efforts to be all I can be for you. There are those available (even for us) in counsel, to help us renew our energies and to help guide us in our work with you.

I have the same opportunities as you to work with the Angels. The big difference is that I have the ability to be directly involved. I can see, hear and feel them, so that is a major help to me... and to you, too. Many of you already have the ability to see, hear, and feel those of us in the Spirit world, and you don't even realize that reality. How sad **that** is.

I am here at this moment to ask you to TRY. Learn to meditate. Guided meditation is excellent for this journey. It helps you to relax. It helps you to visualize more easily by listening and following the voice that is guiding you. If you do not have a guided meditation CD or cassette, there are many places you can purchase them. Metaphysical bookstores, the psychic fairs, and even health food stores will often have them. Your larger bookstores with a metaphysical section will often have them, too. Try your local library, also. (And don't forget the list of meditations in the back of this book that you can order.)

If you try and things don't happen quickly for you, just realize each person has their own 'stuff' to heal. It is in the healing that the little miracles come to pass. You cannot truly know when it is the right time for you to be open enough for the conscious interaction with the Spirit world. It just happens... sometimes quickly, sometimes seemingly painfully slow. But if you will do your part in your efforts to work with us, we will certainly do ours. As Dale says in her own opening to spirit journey... she opened the door, then it seemed like Spirit reached through and jerked her right on in.

The journey might be frightening for some of you, but only because you have your own past to work on. Past life issues, as well as this life's past have to be dealt with. You are not alone in this, even though you may feel you are. I can promise you that your people in spirit are working even harder at helping you get to that space.

We truly have a desire to communicate with all of you on the conscious level. One of the first steps in our journey is to help you all understand that the Universe is one unit, and each of you is a very definite part of that unit.

Now, my interaction with the Angelic world is three-fold:

1) As I work with Dale, I am learning to interact with not only her, but with her clients, also. This is very important for all concerned, because I help deceased loved ones of our clients learn how to communicate with Dale. Oh, many of them are so **not** into doing this. Even though they come to visit with you and try on their own personal level to communicate with you, it is a foreign idea to work through someone they do not know. (We will discuss this in a later chapter.)

2) The Angelic presence as we are working with these deceased loved ones helps add to the strength of the energy so the communication is clearer with all those concerned. When I need help there are the Teacher Angels always near to guide me.

Each of you is very loved and protected by those of us in Spirit that have that ability. I am a Sprite (a person of nature, one who has great love for Mother Earth and all those living things of earth, including YOU). I am not a protector. That is mostly left up to the world of the Guardians.

The Guardians are the Angels and any other individual or group that has the ability to create protective energy for you. I am blessed, as Dale is, to know and interact with these individuals on a conscious level. They are also available to you, whether you are aware of them or not.

Guardians are of various backgrounds. Each of you has a Guardian Angel, but many of you have more protectors than the Angelic world.

These protectors have the ability to create a barrier around you, and to allow only those energies to come near you that are compatible with you. There are Angels available to help you on the earth plain as well as those of us working with you. You must understand, though, that when your path calls for some accident or traumatic experience, the Guardians can**not** interfere. You created that experience before you came into being on the earth plain, and it is some challenge you have to live through for your own reasons. Most of you will not recognize this until you pass into spirit from death of body to review the life you just left.

If you have any negative experience from the spirit world, your own doubts created it. Learn to trust those protectors, know that they have imminent power to create the barrier to keep the negative energies of the universe away from you.

Some of you might experience things you perceive as negative or frightening, that truly are not. Usually, these can be explained by a person already able to work on a deeper level with the Spirit world.

3) There are Healing Angels to help all of us as we live each day. Those of us who work with you while you are on your journey in the denseness of the earth also face some of the hazards you do. We do not tire as you do, and do not have the fears that are so prevalent with you, but we worry about you, and when you are sad... so are we. This can be very draining on us. We go to the Healing Angels to renew our spirit, our energy... and so can you.

Interaction with the Angelic world is a thing we helpers take for granted at times. We are really grateful to know this reality when we see how hard some of you try to break through the veil. You desire on the conscious level to know what is on the other side, yet cannot get to that place as fast as you desire. The Healing Angels work with you as much as you will allow. They help to heal the disappointments and the fears and uncertainties that are often in your life on your journey.

One thing that is very powerful and I want to pass it on to you. If each of you, on a daily basis, would ask your Angels, guides, and loved ones in spirit to join with you to create a healing circle, there would be much less negativity in your world. In your mind, just send out an invitation to anyone near you, asking that they join you in creating a healing circle.

As your circle is formed (use your imagination if you cannot see them or feel them), and know that they (we) will never fail you. The healing circle is magical. Call in people you know are in need of special healing. Sometimes you may even need to put yourself in that circle. Always remember to include Mother Earth in that circle as the healing will benefit many through her.

Reiki, prayer, or just love extended to those you've called into the circle will be a tremendous force for the soul of that person and strength and healing for the human of that soul.

As you finish, say... "I release all energies that are not mine... I call back my own energy." Depending on how open you are to feeling energy... you might even **feel** the releasing of those that are not you, then feel the return of your own energy.

Here is one last thing about working with the Angelic world. I have had occasion to ask for special guidance in one thing or another, and they are always there to help me. YOU must always remember to ask, too. As you have heard, you may not get what you ask for when you want it, and there is a great possibility that you will not recognize the reality of what you receive as what you asked for, but they never let you down.

Chapter 7

Our Work With Lost Souls

The most important thing we do... our work to retrieve the souls of those that, for whatever reason, have not completed their journey 'home'. Home is heaven... the Astral.... that space of love and peace where souls go after death of body.

There are so many reasons a soul might not complete its journey home... just a few of them are suicide, confusion, uncertainty, and fear. But the truth is that no one is ever turned away. God's love is tremendous, and that love welcomes all back home that will come.

We work with those earth bound souls in many ways. One is to *clear houses*, to visit those places that are haunted. Most people don't realize the reason they are able to pick up on the energy of a ghost is because they, themselves, are actually using their own psychic abilities.

Earth bound spirits (or ghosts, as the word most often used) are not typically evil or dangerous. Most are just lonely, desirous of company, and usually quite bored. When a person comes along into their life that has some *knowing* of the spirit... this excites them; it gives them more energy (just as you gain more energy from being excited). They finally have some attention directed to them, even if it's fear. They try harder and harder to do things to keep your attention, to communicate with you.

When we are asked to go to someone's home, business, or property to help 'clear' it, we always go with the intention of using love. Dale has the ability to hear spirit; this is called clairaudience or clear hearing. It is a very valuable gift that many of you have (and that many of you are uncertain about). She uses this gift to communicate with that spirit, helping them to understand that there is a need for them to go home. Just some of the reasons for them to let go of the earth plane are to find peace and healing, love and joy from those waiting for them on the other side of the veil.

My part in this is to stand with Dale, adding to her energy to work with these people. I am able to do this because Michael, our Spirit teacher, creates a special envelope of space that accelerates the ability to interact with them. Not all psychics work in this manner, but Dale decided not to be open and aware of all peoples at all times. She felt it to be an invasion of privacy, but when needed, the space is there automatically.

Realize when you have reached that place in your growth and desire to be available to those earthbound souls, you have much help in connecting with them. We (your own Spirit teachers, Angels, and guides) will allow those spirits to come into your space when it is really needed... for your education, as well as for the sake of that soul.

We have worked with many lost souls, and each of them has their reason for being earthbound. Our first experience in this particular lifetime was with a gentleman named James. He was really a neat person... very unassuming, and quite open to us. He had been decapitated in a boating accident, was drawn to our light, and was allowed in by the protectors.

James first appeared with his head under his arm... it wasn't scary... just a body carrying his head. Dale realized his problem, and since James didn't seem too upset, she laughed at his predicament and asked him if he did not realize he was spirit and could easily be complete. She asked him to return his head to its rightful place and he did so. They talked for a bit and Dale helped him to see his people in spirit that were waiting to guide him home. He has even come to visit a couple of times since then.

The other end of the spectrum was when we were asked to go to a home to help remove a spirit that was terrorizing the family. (Mom and numerous children from early teens to young adult, and a 2 year old granddaughter lived in the home together). The spirit had been waking different members of the family by scratching them, and had actually pushed the baby out of her bed one time. This was the most serious we had encountered so far. Dale prayed for guidance. Arch Angel Michael said to go and to listen to his directions in every move when we got to the home.

When we got there, Michael said to sit in the living room on the couch and ask the ghost to join her. She talked to the spirit, promising that if he would go home and try it, he would not have to stay... he could return to the earth plain if he so desired.... but he would NOT be allowed to return to this home or to terrorize any others. He finally agreed, and as he left, a woman's voice said, "I don't want to stay here alone". His earthly wife had been so dependent on him that even in death of body she had stayed with him. The Angels helped her home to her own freedom.

On our way home Dale asked Michael just what would have happened if the man had not agreed to go, and Michael showed himself holding golden ropes. The spirit would have been bound and taken. As it was… he was taken to a safe place between earth and home... a kind of a half-way-house where he could receive love and healing. Then, after a time, he will be allowed to decide where he truly wants to go.

Choice (free will) is not only a human reality; it is a reality in the spirit world, too. We tend to live our lives in a co-operative way that hurts no one. We care for each other in a similar fashion to the way best of friends care for each other on the earth plane, but we are separate when we desire to be. It is a free will decision when a soul decides to stay on or near the earth plain after death of body. We definitely work with that individual, and we try to help them understand how different their lives would be if they would go to the light, but there is no force to make a change.

When that earth bound soul begins to antagonize others or to hurt them in some way, and if we are asked for help... we help!

Chapter 8

Loved Ones In Spirit

Sometimes, the ghost that is haunting you is a loved one who has not let go of you, or family, or the earth plain. There are too many reasons to mention that this reality occurs. Now, do not confuse a deceased loved one who has stayed earthbound with one that has gone home and has returned to be a guide. They may have returned to share their knowledge and to guide you, another family member, or even a dear friend. This doesn't happen often, but it **does** happen. The energy and feel... the vibration.... of these individuals is totally different.

When we have a client's loved one come forward to give a message, it can be hit or miss. Even though Dale can hear the Spirit world, your loved ones are on a different frequency. She hears OUR world easily because she has been attuned to our frequency and we are in a more clear space. And as she works diligently to continue her journey of healing herself (and as we continue to work **with** her) she hears more and more clearly the words spoken by your loved ones.

When you come to us as a client, sometimes you bring a loved one with you that has already passed into spirit due to death of body. They are especially open to being with you if you have thought to send a message to them about the experience. This does not mean that they are always willing to work with Dale, since she is a total stranger to them. But the really neat thing is that they are usually very excited to have the opportunity to communicate with you.

They do not channel through Dale as we do, but use thought transference and symbols to communicate as well as the energy that they can create to help you know that they are there. Few people are truly open to the 'feel' of the energy of their loved one in spirit, or at least they typically are unable to identify the individual 'feel' of that person's energy. Mainly, they just are silent until we urge them to speak out.

We, Dale's people in Spirit, work as guidance at times, especially when she works with the earth bound souls. These people are lost in so many ways. The question has arisen as to why, when the Angels have so much power, why are humans needed to help these souls to cross over?

The Angels NEVER interfere with a human's or a spirit's desire. Those souls who are earth bound are typically trying to complete some issue they feel is necessary, and some are there because they are so uncertain about where they belong, or might be accepted. These spirits will typically only recognize those of you that are human... they avoid any contact with others in the spirit world. So, it is necessary to employ those of you that are willing to help these souls to find their loved ones that are waiting on them, or see the tunnel of light, or their Angel... or ME!

There is much rejoicing when a long lost (or a short lost soul) comes home to our world. So much can be done in the immediate crossing to help them understand the power of love, and the beauty of our world. It is with joy that we embrace each of you who make the effort to work with us.

One of the things Dale does often helps the client to understand the difference of the energy of the loved one that is earth bound, and the energy after he/she goes home. If you have lost a loved one and that person is almost constantly on your mind, and you do not seem to be healing of the grief of loss... then it is very possible that the soul of the deceased loved one is still earth bound, and staying near you.

In our private sessions, we have time to work with these earth bound souls. Sometimes they let Dale know they are there, because she can sense their energy, but often the client will ask about that deceased loved one. Then Dale can ask the soul to come forward, talk to that soul, and ask why they have chosen to stay on the earth plain. Also, we try to help that soul understand what they are missing by staying on earth. There is the love, understanding of their past and present, beauty, healing, joy, reuniting with passed family members and friends. There is so much that they are missing out on by not going home.

Dale helps that soul to understand they do NOT have to stay at home (spiritual home) if they choose not to. (But we have not had ANY choose to return to the earthbound status, truly!) We help that earthbound soul to create the strength in energy to see those who are waiting for them if they have not already done so. Before they go... Dale will ask that soul to give a hug to the client (this is hardly ever refused by the client). The hug is a dense or rather heavy feel, according to Dale. When a client gets a hug from spirit, we ask them to just be aware of any change inside or out... warm, cool, tingle... they might even feel a gentle hug.

Then, she asks the soul to come right back after going through the veil, and give another hug to the client. (When the loved one returns to give the second hug... the energy is much less dense.) She asks the soul to give the hugs for two reasons. One is that the client can often actually FEEL the energy change of the deceased loved one before and after going home. It shows the client some of the possibilities of contact. Another is to help the soul realize they really CAN come back to the earth plane to visit if they desire to. That fear of leaving loved ones behind on the earth plain with no contact does seem to be a hindrance to some of them moving on to their true home in the spirit world.

All in all, we truly love our work in this area... it is very rewarding, and one of the very best ways to help the soul, the client, AND Mother Earth to heal. You see, and this may be a bit hard to understand, the fewer souls that are earth bound, the lighter the energy and frequency of earth. The many earthbound souls add to the negativity because they are like shadows of fear, confusion and uncertainty. This is part of what you and we are trying to heal.

Chapter 9
Tools Of Our Trade

A Joy Guide who has too many duties can truly overload her/himself, so we have to pick and choose exactly what we desire to create with our human. This is not at all a thing that might create uncertainty... it is truly a joyful experience to work with our human in deciding what we can best create together.

For instance, Dale and I decided long ago we would concentrate on the spirit world and do what we could to help them reconnect with their loved ones still on earth. When a client has created an appointment to visit with us, they usually have some reason in mind. If that reason is to just find out about relationships, finances, business, etc., they usually do not send out the message to any relatives or friends in spirit that they desire to meet with them.

In that case, usually only their Angels and guides will come to the session with them. We are always looking for an opportunity to communicate with you. Sometimes, you will bring a loved one with you without realizing it. They might get Dale's attention if they have something to say, but usually they will impress upon YOU the idea to ask about them.

If you create an appointment with us specifically to visit with a loved one in spirit, then that person will usually know this and will meet with you at that time. You see, your thoughts of that loved one in spirit sends out a vibration that is recognized and read by them, and you will receive some kind of response. They will meet with you if at all possible, and if they cannot, they will send a member of their own party to take their place.

In actuality, the most important thing they desire to express to you during the visit is that they are alive and well, that the love for each of you still on the earth plane has even increased, and yet it is different. They will often be so full of excitement at the meeting, it can overwhelm the medium present and the words can sometimes become confusing.

When you have a specific question for them or about them, ask it. Don't play guessing games with them or the medium. The spirit you are connecting with is the same, yet they do not connect with your concerns as you do. They realize the worries while on earth are just that, and often will release those concerns to a great degree as they re-enter home.

Yes, they will carry the effects of much of what they experienced while on earth, but they are learning how to deal with these on a different level than you. Some of you will hear and feel the same Mom, Dad, Uncle John, or Aunt Jane you knew well while they were there with you in body. But occasionally, we have experienced a loved one who tried to express the person they have grown into since death of body.

So many of you feel that those deceased loved ones never change... they stay the same person/personality that they were while on the earth plain. This is far from the truth. Just as you continue to grow and change while on earth... so will you after death of body.

Occasionally, a loving relative will take the position of Joy Guide. When this happens, it is really exciting for that person in spirit because of the complexities we are faced with. It means that relative is definitely an older soul, with a fascination for discovering the many different ways of helping their human to evolve.

When you are depressed or in trouble and the energy in and around you is very heavy... we, as Joy Guides, are the ones usually the closest to you. Yes, we do try to cheer you up, but we also try to reason with you. You, too, have a responsibility to us. You must do all you can to help get **yourself** out of that space. We cannot do it alone!

Certain traits are required of us to work directly with you. A bland personality just will not do, so you can expect your Joy Guide to be out-going, positive, loving, energetic, and as we said earlier... sometimes incorrigible (but that part is all in the name of good fun and trying to get you to recognize us!). We do have a few that are quite shy when you first learn about them on the conscious level, but it doesn't take long for them to return to the gregarious personality needed for the job.

We do not work alone. There is a major network of people who are a part of your life, and the amazing thing to us is that most of you go through whole lifetimes not even aware of us.

We are sad when you are frightened of us, but given today's reality of the sensationalism of some books that are written and movies created just to see who and what can scare people the most... we certainly understand the fear. On top of that, many of you have the cell memories of past life atrocities that instill a fear in you, even though you do not understand where it comes from.

Those fears are a major challenge to you AND to us in helping you to open up to our world. Even those of you who have a great conscious desire to interact with us will have a rough time doing so if you do not actively work at healing your fears and uncertainties. There are many ways to discover those fears. Past life regression will often help you to release and heal. A meditation you can work on in your own time and privacy is what we call "The Healing Mountain".

The Healing Mountain

Close your eyes, and take a few deep breaths to relax. In your mind or out loud, ask to see your fears about your psychic abilities (or the spirit world or any other goal) represented by a dark mountain in front of you.

Use your imagination (your third eye) to see this dark mountain. Let it grow to whatever size it will (that will show you the size of the barrier you've created to that goal). You might see a mountain range instead of a mountain. You might see only black (that usually means the mountain is so huge that you can't see around it!). You might create something besides a mountain.... something that **you** subconsciously want to represent the barrier you've created to that goal.

Open your heart like a big beautiful open rose right in the middle of your chest, and send your mountain lots of love (that mountain is your child, your creation from your stuff that needs to be healed). Ask God to send your mountain lots of love and light, and ask your Angels,

Teachers, Guides, and loved ones in spirit to send your mountain lots of love and healing energy.

Watch your mountain begin to change to light energy, and as it is disappearing, you will eventually feel that healing energy flow into the chakras (energy centers) of your body affected by negative energy.

Work with this mountain often. You are like an onion with many different layers… as you heal one layer, another will eventually surface with a similar need.

You can also use this tool to work with your negativity. If you feel bad, angry, depressed - any perceived negative emotion - ask every part of yourself to release that negative energy. PUSH it out of yourself and let it form that dark mountain. Then just follow the directions above to help heal the issue.

When you are consciously active in trying to heal yourself, you will move ahead to your goals much more quickly than just letting nature take its course.

Chapter 10

More Tools

We are proudest of the healing tools that we help Dale create for herself, for clients and students, and for YOU. There are so many ways for each of you to help yourself, but the biggest problem is that most of you will not take the time to work with the ideas you read about, hear about, or even the ones that come to you in your own minds.

When Dale learns about a way to help heal the self, she usually takes the time to experiment with it. For instance, when you are reading a book, and there are directions on how to feel energy or a meditation, then stop right there. Follow the instructions and see what you can feel, hear, smell, or see. You'll find that it is most beneficial to learn to read in this manner, and you'll be surprised at how quickly you'll begin to open to those experiences. Of course, it takes longer to finish a book when you do this, but you'll find it well worth the time.

If it feels right, and helps her in any way, she puts it on tape, CD, or in a file. The most helpful are often used to help with her self-growth, and in sharing with others. Most stumbling blocks to success are based on fear, which often creates confusion, which then creates problems in further action to any goal. Dale uses the following exercise often to help banish blocks and barriers to success in any area of her life and to clear confusion.

It is really easy to do this if you are clairaudient (have clear hearing), but even if you do not, you can still be quite successful, and will be amazed at how much change you can create within the self and in your life.

We will assume you do not already recognize the voices of your teachers in spirit, or communicate with the different parts of the self yet. So, all you have to do is listen to your own thoughts.

Find a comfortable place to write. It is important to put this on paper, and to even create a file for your visits within, so you might go back and see where you were in the beginning compared to where you will be in a few months or years.

<u>Working With and Knowing the Different Parts of Self</u>
Shared with you by Dale and Daisy

Mental Body

Physical Body

Emotional Body

Chatter-box (The little voice in your head that seems to talk all the time.)

Sub-Conscious

Soul Incarnate

Ego

Heart

Spiritual Body

These are energies within yourself that you can actively work with to heal issues of the past and present.

Getting to know and love these parts (or facets) of yourself is important because it is very strengthening and healing. It will help to create a strong foundation on which to build your future.

The chakras and the different facets of the self we are now introducing to you have a direct influence on the health of the physical body. Those of you that have worked with chakras might have a deeper understanding of this presentation.

Chakras function as bridges between the body and universal energy. The energy taken in through each chakra is sent to different parts of the body.

Remember that you, as human, are made up of many different energies, which we are calling 'parts' or 'facets' of the self. In working with these different facets, you are actually working directly with the chakra system and your energy field, helping to enhance your total health and well being.

Some of the following information about the Chakras is from: "Light Emerging" by Barbara Ann Brennan.

#1: 1st Chakra (Root Chakra) interaction with Physical Body and Mental Body:
Located at the base of the spine,

Purpose – Survival or Will to Live
Focus – Grounding
Color – Red
Psychological Functioning – Survival
Gland – Adrenal
Areas of Body Governed – Spinal Column, Kidneys, Nervous System, Feet, Legs

#2: 2nd Chakra (Sacral Center) interaction with Physical, Emotional, and Mental Bodies: Located mid-sacral lower abdomen, below the navel

Purpose – Desire, Pleasure & Reproduction
Focus – Will to Feel, to be Emotional
Color – Orange, Tangerine
Psychological Functioning – Desire & Sexuality
Glands – Gonads
Areas of Body Governed – Reproductive System, Lower Abdomen

#3: 3rd Chakra (Solar Plexus) interaction with Physical, Emotional, and Mental Bodies and Ego: Located in the solar plexus area on the front and back of the body, between the belly button and breastbone.

Purpose – Seat of the Ego – Self Interest, Intuition, Related to who we are in the Universe, how we take care of ourselves, how we connect with others.
Focus – Will to Think (mental) & Clearing Lower Centers
Color – Yellow
Psychological Functioning – Will resulting in power
Gland – Pancreas

Areas of Body Governed – Stomach, Liver, Gall Bladder, Upper Abdomen, Spleen, Nervous System

#4: 4th Chakra (Heart Chakra) interaction with Spiritual and Emotional Bodies and Heart.: Located in the heart area, in the center of the chest and is related to love and will. The front chakra is related to love, and the back chakra is related to will.

Purpose – Transformer
Focus – Love & Radiance
Color – Green, (we include pink and mauve)
Psychological Functioning – Love resulting in balance
Gland – Thymus
Areas of Body Governed – Heart, Blood, Circulatory System, Arms, Chest, Hands, Upper Back, Vagus Nerve.

#5: 5th Chakra (Throat Chakra) interaction with Mental and Emotional Bodies, Chatter, and Subconscious: Located at the front and back of the throat, and is associated with the sense of hearing, tasting, and smelling.

Purpose – Will to Express
Focus – Higher Emotions
Color – Blue
Psychological Functioning – Communication, Giving & Receiving
Gland – Parathyroid & Thyroid
Areas of Body Governed – Bronchial, Vocal, Lungs, Ears, Respiratory System

#6: 6th Chakra (Brow Chakra) interaction with Mental and Spiritual Bodies:
Located between eyebrows, at the center of the brow and back of the head.

Purpose – The Seat of the Mind & the Center of the Brow
Focus – Visioning, Compassion, & Wisdom
Color – Indigo
Psychological Functioning – Intuition & Imagination
Gland – Pituitary
Areas of Body Governed – Lower Brain, Eyes, Nose, Nervous System. (The front chakra is related to conceptual understanding, and the back one is related to carrying out our ideas in a step by step process to accomplish them.)

#7: 7th Chakra (Crown Chakra) interaction with Spiritual Body and Soul:

Located at the top of the head with the larger end of the vortex pointed upward.

Purpose – The Seat of the Soul
Focus – Higher Will or Knowing
Color – Violet / White
Psychological Functioning – Understanding, Oneness, Knowing, Related to the Integration of Personality and Spirituality
Gland – Pineal
Areas of Body Governed – Upper Brain

Most of you have been taught from a very early age to love others and to do for others before yourself, but how can you truly be all you can be if you don't create this for yourself first.

The first step is to introduce yourself to each part (or facet) of self. Close your eyes and use your imagination... take a deep breath and relax. Imagine that your heart is like a big beautiful flower right in the middle of your chest (that's where the heart chakra is). Let that flower begin to open... let it open completely.

Using your imagination (third eye), imagine that the different parts of the self are like children... small replicas of yourself... and they are starved for love and attention. Imagine that as each of them stand in front of you, you are sending lots of love, then ask that part of self to put his/her arms around your neck and imagine giving a big, loving hug to each other. As you do this, that facet melts back inside of you.

IMPORTANT: do this with each of the nine facets of the self.

You can begin with any one of the facets... and there is no particular order to follow. For instance, ask Heart to step outside the body to receive love from you, your Angels, guides, and loved ones in spirit. *SEE* Heart as that small replica (child) of you, imagine embracing that child in your arms for a hug. See if you can *FEEL* this happening.

They may be timid at first, but the more you work with them in this manner, the safer and more comfortable they will be about creating this experience. If you continue to work at healing yourself, you will be able to feel movement in and around you in time.

The next phase can be done now or at a later time.

Ask each facet of the self to write out its goals, joys, fears, anger... whatever it desires to talk about. Just allow thoughts to surface in your mind and write them down under or beside the name of that facet. There may be much similarity, but you will be surprised at how different some of the information can be from them. Ask what fears have been brought into this life from the past... see what is said.

YOU MUST TRUST YOUR THOUGHTS, even if it does not seem to fit with your present reality, you might go back and read what is written at a later time, and understand it more.

The next phase can be done at a later time, also... and this one will be helpful if you will use it often (as the hugs above will).

Create your round table of self (an imaginary round table, with an imaginary chair for each part of the self). From time to time you might ask one of your teachers in spirit to join this round table, but it is important to allow the different facets of self to answer first. You'll understand why as we explain.

Write down a question that you wish an answer to... maybe something you have been wrestling with or have been undecided about. (See guideline on the next page.) Allow each facet of the self to answer this question. For example... under the question, write 'Heart'... then allow heart to speak. If there is any fear, uncertainty, or **any** negative answer (or thought)... ask God to send a counselor to work with that facet of you and go on to the next facet of self. Allow it to answer the question, then return later to the one that worked with the counselor to understand any change in its answer.

You also might ask if this negativity was brought into today's life from a past life. Often, you have fears and uncertainties in your life that you have no idea of where they came from. If it is a past life problem, just look at it in today's reality. For instance, if you have a desire to use your own psychic abilities more, and seem unable to reach your goals, you might have been persecuted or even murdered in another life because of your psychic or healing abilities. This would create a deep-seated fear in you of bringing it into your reality again in today's world. Recognizing that it was based on a past experience and that using these abilities today is safe will do a lot to help release that barrier or limitation and continue your growth.

Another example... Dale had worked at a particular place for 20 years, was making a good salary, but was not happy there anymore. It was a rather dead-end job, and she was unable to find a suitable place for her talents. She had been trying for a few years to get brave enough to leave that place of business, but was within 10 years of retirement, and had all the major benefits, etc.

Our spirit teacher, Michael, had asked Dale to leave that job... to work full time as a psychic/healer. Dale felt she had too much to lose if she left that position. One day, she found the book, "Channeling" (an Experiential Guide for the Channel) by Vywamus at a local bookstore. Vywamus is a spirit teacher that channeled the book, and comes with the book if you desire his presence, and will work with you if you ask. In reading it, she discovered the idea for the round table, worked with that idea, and built it into even more over the years.

OUR miracle in this experience was that after only two weeks of working with her round table, and concentrating on healing her fears about leaving that job... she turned in her resignation.

And here we are...hopeful that each of you can find as much strength in making decisions and going forward in your own journey as she has!

The following example will give you an idea about how to work with the different facets of the self on paper. Use it as a guideline, but when you work with your roundtable the facets do not have to be in any particular order.

(This technique is taught in our workshop "Body, Mind, & Soul Connection.") Please turn to the next page to begin.

QUESTION (write your question):

_____

_____

ANSWER FROM EACH FACET OF SELF

MENTAL:

_____

_____

_____

_____

_____

PHYSICAL:

_____

_____

_____

_____

_____

CHATTER:

_____

_____

_____

_____

_____

EMOTIONAL BODY:

_____

_____

_____

_____

_____

EGO:

_____

_____

_____

_____

_____

HEART:

_____

_____

_____

_____

_____

SOUL:

_____

_____

_____

_____

_____

SUB-CONSCIOUS:

_____

_____

_____

_____

_____

SPIRITUAL BODY:

_____

_____

_____

_____

_____

Chapter 11

Daffodils & Marigolds

Fields of flowers... rainbows of pure, true color... people of love, and people of light. All these things you possess on the earth plane. What a joy to be able to express pure joy... what an effort it is sometimes.

Each of you has the inherent ability to remove limitations... to heal yourself. We are here to help guide you, but WE are the ones that are limited... especially if you don't even make an effort to allow us to help.

It is my greatest joy to work with you, to share with you in all our abundance of experiences that help you, others, and us in some way. These experiences are often unnoticed by you, and yet we keep trying over and over to get your attention. But when you DO recognize the abundance of life... and especially when you DO recognize our presence and help... oh, how exciting it is for us in spirit.

Occasionally, you will stray or believe in some part of the self that has emerged in fear or uncertainty. When this happens, we do all we can to clear the energy of negativity away... we create our healing circle around you... especially when you are sleeping. We pray for the uncertainty to dissipate, but we can not do it alone... when you go into a negative mode, YOU have to work at healing yourself, too.

There are those people that hardly recognize the beauty that is available all around them. We ask each of you to begin a new and exciting journey. Start a journal! It doesn't have to be a daily one, but if you would write down all the really neat, wonderful, beautiful things that come into your life...you would be creating **more** really neat, wonderful, beautiful things in your life. Don't you realize that like attracts like? As you start observing and feeling more of the positive, you are actually creating more of it in your life.

Sometimes a negative energy will hang on to you for a very long period of time. Depression is a major concern of ours for those of you on the earth plain because it makes you close in on yourself. Often the depressed person doesn't have the energy to do anything about it. But,

I tell you right now... if you try, you will win that war of dark and light... you can be the light.

The medical practitioners of the earth plain are there ready to give you something that will make you sleep or slow down your energy even more. Occasionally, you'll find someone that really understands that to fight depression, you need light, laughter, and love.

Those of you with chemical imbalances are truly in need of medication.... always follow your doctor's advice. But we ask you to begin your own regimen of healing, too. Change your diet to a really healthy one, get out and get exercise... even if it's just a walk around the block. Protect your skin, but sit in the sunshine for awhile as often as possible. Dig in the dirt, plant flowers... daffodils and marigolds... joy in the spring, and joy in the summer.

YOU HAVE TO CHANGE YOUR ATTITUDE ABOUT LIFE. If you are having an excessive amount of problems, whether it is personal, business, spiritual or anything else doesn't matter. What matters is the attitude you have toward those problems. I, Daisy, personally guarantee that things will get better for you if you just make a change in the way you perceive any given problem.

Did you know that when you pray, if we happen to be near, we join you in prayer?? We do. And did you know that if you ask us to join you in prayer, we are overjoyed. And did you know that if you ask us to pray for you or another... we take the time to do so. And did you know that whether you realize it or not.... YOU are always in our prayers, too.

I speak for your people in spirit, not just for me. I am their spokesperson right now, and this is really important for you to realize that we do these things. We **feel** your joys, your pain... whatever you experience is expressed in your energy field. When you are hurting mentally, physically, or emotionally... it's a very distressful thing for those of us that love you.

It is OUR job to be available to do what we can to help you through the life you have created for yourself on the earth plain. It is a job of love... what could be finer??

In an effort to help you understand that we are a reality, to understand a little bit of our duties with you, I take pride in the ability to communicate with you in this way. But I ask each of you to begin the journey to work with and to communicate with your Joy Guide. It might not be in the same way that I communicate with Dale, but you and your Joy Guide will find a way if you are willing.

Clairaudience is not at all a necessary ingredient to working with your people in spirit. There are many ways of connecting with us, and if you have not made the effort (or if you have, and feel you have failed)... please don't give up. It often takes a lot of patience **and persistence** to break through your own barriers. We have that patience and persistence, and we pray that you do, too.

Chapter 12

Meditation For Meeting Your Joy Guide

You might want to create your own cassette to listen to for a guided meditation to meet your Joy Guide, or just allow this one for guidance. If you desire one already on tape... see the appendix in the back of this book on how to order this guided meditation or the others that are available.

Find a comfortable place to relax for a little while. Make sure you will not be disturbed... **you** can decide for how long.

Close your eyes, and take three or four deep breaths... breath in through the nose and out the mouth. As you do this, allow your body to release all tension, and just relax more and more with each breath released.

Feel Mother Earth supporting you, cradling you as you feel a warm loving energy beginning in your feet... flowing into your ankles... relaxing, releasing all stress... and continuing to flow into the calves, knees, and thighs of your legs. Then on into the hips and lower back... feel this wonderfully relaxing energy flow right on through your torso touching and expanding your heart...

Continuing to breathe deeply... feel this energy flow into your shoulders... relaxing, releasing all that tension... on into your arms, wrists, hands, fingers... Now, feel the warmth in the shoulders and flowing into the muscles of the neck... (relax, relax)... into the scalp, forehead, eyes, and the muscles of the face......

As you have released all that stress, relaxing all the parts of your body, your energy field is getting more and more clear. The colors of the energy field around you are vibrant; see if you can see any colors in your mind's eye.

Now, using your imagination (the gateway to your third eye experiences) create a place for yourself... a safe, beautiful place... could be inside or outside, in a meadow, by a lake or stream...in a forest... it doesn't matter at all... this is YOUR place and you can visit it any time you desire.

Find a place to just sit or lie down... a place of comfort for YOU. Now, in your mind, call out for your Joy Guide to come visit with you and wait a moment or two.

As you look around at your special place... you notice a small light beginning to grow bigger and bigger near you... just like a spotlight shining on a stage. Now, as you are watching that light... you begin to see a figure take form.

Do you see any special colors? Write down or remember exactly how things are unfolding right before your eyes. Is your Joy Guide a girl, a boy, or has your guide decided to show you some kind of small cuddly animal??

Talk to your Joy Guide... you may not hear the words... but pay attention to your thoughts. Do not doubt... write down your thoughts, what you hear, what you see, what you feel.

Ask your Joy Guide for his or her name. Trust.

Feel the energy around your Joy Guide... talk for a bit... ask for a message...

It's time to return to the present, so say good-by for now, and know that you can return here again and again.

In time, you will just automatically connect with your Joy Guide in your thoughts without creating your safe place.

Now, as I count to 5... I want you to begin to be aware of your surroundings.

One... two... (Feel the energy of the present time and place begin to come into your awareness)... three (feel the blood flow through your body... awakening you to **new** energy)... four (begin to move your body to awaken it even more to the present)... five (you are now fully awake)!

BLESSINGS TO EACH AND EVERY ONE OF YOU... I AM DAISY, AND THIS IS NOT JUST MY JOURNEY WITH YOU... IT IS YOUR OWN JOY GUIDE'S GIFT TO YOU AND TO THEM!!

Client's/Student's
Experiences

Kyle Pierce, Louisville, KY.

One day, during a particularly deep meditation, I was so beautifully approached and hugged by what I thought was an angel. It took me by surprise but was so clear and so perfect, that I just relished in the contact. The clearest image was the white, flowing clothing, tied by a most beautiful golden rope. I didn't see a face, just the torso. It was amazing and I felt so honored and loved.

Soon after this, I met with you (Dale) for a reading. You named 'Poppy' as someone who I knew well and was with me often. I had no idea who this was... you asked more questions and felt sure I knew 'Poppy'. I think that you even mentioned that he comforted or hugged me. Not until you mentioned the beautiful golden rope belt, did it all make sense to me. I don't think Poppy is an angel, but spirit. I ask Poppy for help often now and trust the messages he brings to me.

❧

Jan Scarbrough, Louisville, KY.

(An author of great love and understanding of human nature and possibilities of love and life.)

Taken from her blog (http://www.janscarbrough.com) of October 30,2008.

When the e-mail announcing the Mediumship Development workshop arrived in my inbox, I decided to invest the money and time to find out what it was all about. TV shows like **Medium** staring Patricia Arquette and **Ghost Whisperer** starring Jennifer Love Hewitt have popularized the idea of talking to "spirits".

51

I had met the instructor Dale Epley at a psychic fair several years ago and later sat with her for a couple of readings. I found what Dale told me was "right on".

Last Saturday, I spent the day in her Mediumship class and some of the highlights are:

1) Don't let the word 'metaphysical' disturb you. It simply means that which is beyond the physical... it refers to the mental, emotional, and spiritual phases of man's nature. You are metaphysical. Every time you use your mind to think and your emotions to feel, you are using what lies 'beyond the physical' realm of your five senses, and you are being metaphysical. (From **The Prosperity Secrets of the Ages** by Catherine Ponder.)

2) You are more than you realize. All of us have an innate ability to communicate with people in spirit. You just need the desire to learn and the more you practice, the better you will get.

3) A message from Dale's teacher and patron Michael Darius, a facet of the energy of Arch Angel Michael, explained more: *"It is my wish that each of you begins to understand that YOU are spirit. YOU are able to connect with the unseen world of spirit in communication in many ways. That YOU have the ability already to do this... all that is needed is to open the door between you and that unseen world, and to help you step through without uncertainty or fear."*

4) A medium (mediator, go between) is sensitive to vibrations from the spirit world and is able to convey messages from that world. You become a medium by choice; your teachers and guides never force you or even make the decision to communicate with you.

5) Unlike in the television shows, mediums don't necessarily work with departed souls or ghosts as we popularly know them. A medium can channel energy from angels, guides and teachers in Spirit. It's important to know that these entities are an aspect of the presence of God in our lives.

6) Meditation is an important tool to help you clear away your stress, anger or fear... things that block your ability to channel or that might even make you ill. We practiced several meditations

which I had trouble doing. I was unsure of myself, and although Dale assured me there was no right or wrong, I was still timid.

7) Dale gave us several techniques to try that may help you get started. The first thing you do, when you begin to work with one of your guides, teachers or Angels, is to pray a prayer of protection… something like" "God, thank you for your love and protection". You do not pray to those you are trying to communicate with because they are a part of your 'team'.

8) One exercise we tried was called automatic writing. That was my favorite one because I AM a writer. This kind of 'automatic' writing is when you allow energy from the invisible world to intervene in your hand and arm so that you write on paper information you have no way of knowing from formal education of life experiences.

9) I didn't have much luck doing this during class, but when I tried it in the quiet of my home, I received this response: *'Go forth and see the spotlight. It will come. Be happy. Don't worry. I am your mentor. I am your friend. Believe in me. Trust me. I am your guide'.* Then I asked for a name: *'Peter.'* I asked what he was here to help me do: *'Live life.'* Do you have anything to tell me? *'I want to tell you, you can do this.'*

10) It's a start. I'm encouraged.

In the final exercise of the workshop, we paired up and tried reading for our partner. I quickly found how much of a novice I truly was. I didn't know how to start, and was uncertain that I actually 'heard' or 'saw' anything worth reporting. I know I wasn't open to the communication like I should have been, whether because of natural reticence or inexperience. Everyone at the workshop encouraged me and urged me to continue practicing.

I left that day determined to keep trying, hoping that with practice I can learn to communicate with my spirit guides, teachers and Angels that are here to help me.

Debbie Haffner, Loveland, OH.

(Debbie is a sensitive. She has strong mediumship abilities and has lived in homes in the past that were haunted. She has helped many lost souls to return to their heavenly homes.)

{History of house: The exact year of construction couldn't be determined, but it was sometime during the late 1800's or early 1900's. The entire area is made up of old houses which were built for some type of a private community. In addition to the 25+ houses, the community had its own hotel and its own church (both are now used as private residences). The house my sons own had once been used as an orphanage. During the mobster days, Al Capone and his associates used the hotel and these houses as a refuge/hideout. There are still some existing underground tunnels below this community area.}

When my two bachelor sons were in their early 20's, they decided to buy their 1st house together. As soon as the loan cleared, the previous owners met them at the house, handed them the key and said, "Oh, by the way, the house is haunted". The previous owners left the house in a hurry and it was not just messy, it was a disaster! They had left behind most of their furniture, blankets, dishes, tools, and even a lot of antiques and personal clothing. Toys, papers, garbage and dirty dishes were scattered everywhere... to the point that you could barely walk through the rooms. It took weeks to get it thoroughly cleaned and organized. In the basement my sons found layers of debris from the past as they cleaned the home. The layers contained turn of the century school desks, old religious books, antique woodworking tools, World War II Medic equipment and a lot of 1940-1950 items. It looked like no one had cleaned the basement for several decades.

My sons moved in the same day they received the key. After they spent the first night in the house, my oldest son called me and told me the house was haunted. He wasn't scared or worried because (as a child) he had lived in a few haunted houses with me and he understood that 'ghosts' just need to be helped up. However, after a few nights, he became concerned and asked me to please come over to check it out.

The first time I walked into the house I felt lightheaded (like I was on strong prescription pain medicine). I found it almost impossible to think clearly. My sons showed me the 1st floor (living room, dining room and kitchen) and then took me upstairs to show me the 3 bedrooms. I felt overwhelmed by the presence of 'spirits' but couldn't seem to focus enough to get a sense of who was there. I told my sons I believed there was more than one entity in the house. Then we went toward the basement where he had sensed the strongest presence.

As soon as I grabbed the door knob to the basement, I felt a negative presence. I opened the door, took a couple of steps forward and felt extreme hostility, at the same time I heard a voice (in my head) which said, "Get out!" The energy level was so intense that I took two steps backwards before I even knew I had moved. As I gathered my strength and courage, I went down the steps and half way into the large basement.

The anger seemed to permeate the entire downstairs. I talked to the spirit, but sensed that it wasn't going to listen to anything I said. I retreated back to the upstairs, quite unnerved. I had previously dealt with unhappy or angry spirits, but had never felt such deep hatred.

Over the next few months, my sons and I continued trying to help the spirits, and I feel that my oldest son was successful with several of them. Every time I entered the house, I still had difficulty focusing which made it hard to accomplish things I had planned.

The spirit in the basement identified himself as Daniel, and he often traveled throughout the house. I began to wonder if Daniel was using fear to keep the other spirits from leaving. I never sensed any other spirits in the basement besides Daniel, but it was definitely the most fearful place in the house. No one wanted to go down there.

Different people sensed, saw and heard different things in different parts of the house. Frequently, items went missing only to turn up in strange locations. Sometimes, late at night, people inside the house heard a strange noise coming from outside in front of the house. It sounded like an old wagon being pulled by running horses on cobblestones.

Over the next few years, both sons had their girlfriends move in and eventually my 4 granddaughters were born and lived there. Some people in the house experienced fear, some became angry, and some became deeply depressed. One person had suicidal thoughts. No one slept very well and arguments occurred frequently. Everyone's moods and emotions seemed to be highly intensified and no one could spend any length of time in the house without feeling some type of extreme emotion or agitation. I had to fight alternating feelings of apathy and fear. One of my sons began drinking heavily. I sensed that Daniel was "feeding" off the energy of others.

Of all the rooms in the house, only one bedroom upstairs felt peaceful... though I sensed the presence of a male spirit, who I thought might have been a minister during his lifetime. The kitchen and living room on the 1st level sometimes felt okay, but felt hostile at others. The basement always felt evil. Strange noises (footsteps, doors slamming, a creaking rocking chair, muffled voices, thuds and bangs) were frequently heard throughout the house and could not be identified by rational explanations.

My sons started painting and remodeling the house and it seemed to be making things worse. One day the circuit breaker kicked off again. I started down the basement steps to turn it back on. On the 4th step going down, Daniel literally lifted me up in the air to where only the tips of my toes were touching the steps. I shouted, "NO!" He put me back down so suddenly that I had to struggle to keep my balance. I was so scared that my legs were shaking, so I went back into the kitchen to calm down. I prayed to God to protect me and forced myself to go back to the basement to turn the electric back on. I was relieved that nothing happened this time.

I realized that I needed to find someone with much stronger abilities and a deeper understanding than I had. God was protecting us but my experience wasn't strong enough to deal with Daniel or to convince the other remaining spirits to go up. I didn't really have any idea who I could call. I had already contacted a local psychic that I trusted, but had been told they didn't have experience in this type of situation and didn't know of anyone else I could call. Catholic Priests had a long waiting list and I had deep reservations about asking them for help. I knew of no other ministers I could go to. Even in this day and age, many people think you're crazy if you talk about hauntings.

Then one day while praying to God to please help me find help, Dale's name popped into my head. She had given me two previous readings in the past. Though I didn't really know her, her readings had been very accurate. For several days I resisted the urge to call Dale because she lived two hours away, but her name kept coming to my mind. Finally, I called her. She told me not to tell her any specific details about the house because she would like to get them herself.

On the day Dale came, she first wanted to walk around the outside of the house. As my husband and I walked with Dale, she stopped on the side of the house at a large, plain rock my son had uncovered when he was doing some yard work. Dale told us someone had been buried there in an underground storage facility. I knew then that Dale was going to be able to help us because I had sensed someone had been buried there. Dale told us there were underground catacombs all through the area which made it easy for spirits to travel into and out of the house. She stopped frequently and told us Michael was sealing all of the catacombs shut so the spirits could not travel through them. After we circled the house, we went inside.

As we walked through the house, Dale, Daisy (her Joy Guide), and Michael worked with numerous spirits and helped them to the Light. As we went toward the kitchen, Dale was quiet for a minute and said we wouldn't need to go into the basement. She began to talk to the spirit who had come up from the basement. When she asked him his name he wouldn't respond. She asked several more times and then turned to us and chuckled. She told us that he had said she could call him "Poison". Dale told Poison (Daniel), "You can go peacefully or be bound and removed by Michael. It's your choice." He left without being bound.

Later, Dale told us Michael would be taking Daniel to a type of 'halfway house' for spirits that were not ready to completely return to their Spiritual Home.

Next, we walked into the hallway near the front door. There is an antique set of double doors that slide sideways into the walls. Dale stopped next to the doors and said she saw a young man wearing a cap and knickers' length shorts with suspenders. When she described the 1940 style of cloths, I instantly knew they were 'Gangster' style. I then told her about this area having been a 'hideout' area for Al Capone and his associates.

Dale mentioned that clearing this house had given her new experiences. I was impressed with how calm and peaceful she was. Her strong faith and lack of fear enabled her to succeed in helping us and the spirits. There were a total of eight spirits helped up that day by Dale, Daisy and Michael.

Recently, when I was putting together this story, my step-daughter (who was 14 at the time and baby-sitting with my granddaughters in one of the adjoining rooms) told me it had been very weird for her. She said that the air had felt tense and thick and then all of a sudden the heavy feeling was just gone. I had felt the effect of Daniel's (a.k.a. Poison) leaving in the exact same way.

There aren't words to adequately describe the difference in the feeling of the house after Dale's visit. Immediately after she left and still to this day, there are no more footsteps, doors slamming, voices, shadows, or rocking chair noises. The hostility and feeling like you were being watched is gone as are the nightmares we often experienced while sleeping in the house. It no longer bothers any of us to go down into the basement… nothing of this nature has bothered anyone in the house since that day.

Even though the house has the same lighting as before, it actually looks much brighter. It 'felt' as if we were walking in darkness and someone came in and turned on floodlights. The air felt thick before with fear, anger, depression, intimidation, hostility and negative emotions. When I'm in the house now, the emotions I feel are normal… not ones inflicted upon me by negative energy. My only regret is that I waited so long to contact Dale for help. We went through almost five long years and it only took Dale around an hour to clear the house.

Before I went to bed that night, I asked God to please send special blessings to Dale, Michael, and Daisy (as well as to any others who helped out that day). They truly helped me and my family in our time of need.

Postscript:

(**Dale**) The release of those individuals that were in this home was a very important step to my understanding of the energies I work with in clearing houses. The very essence of those that were involved were changed... not only those spirits that were in the home, but of those humans that lived or visited there.

I did not realize the extent that was explained by Debbie until she wrote this description from her point of view. I am grateful for Michael's love and protection as we walk through the energy that needs to be cleared.

(**Daisy**): My intention in any of the house or business clearings is to simply be there to help where I can. My energy is often needed as a 'stabilizer'... one that helps create a positive 'envelope' of energy to work in.

(**Michael**): As this was a home in need of much preparation, I thank Debbie for her persistence before we even arrived. Her efforts created a proper energetic field for us to work in, otherwise we would not have been able to complete the clearing as quickly as we did.

In an effort to understand the major problem... there was in existence an energetic negative vortex (an opening between dimensions) near the center of the basement that allowed those 'ghosts' movement. This is the reason for so many individual spirits inhabiting the home. Daniel's energy was so potent that once a lost soul wandered into the home, he would not allow them to leave. As some of the souls were children's, he did enjoy tormenting them and using them to create more fear in the adult souls that were in the home.

Also, since Debbie and most of her family were so familiar with interacting with lost souls, it encouraged Daniel to challenge their authority... it became a game of 'wills and strength'.

This was a vastly different reality than most that we have encountered, and we are very thankful that the property has retained its clarity.

Memories of Other House Clearings

Dale, 2007: I had a call for help from a young woman that described the mounting fear she and her friends were having in the apartment they were living in.

I prepare for house clearings with prayer and trust. This puts me in the right space of energy for working as a bridge for Michael and the Angels, Daisy and any other of the entities needed for clearing a property.

As I neared the apartment complex, I noticed they were in an area that was rather run down. The apartments were in need of repair and the area could have used a good cleaning from a human clean-up crew. The reason this is important is that when you are living in poverty, often the negative energy is very powerful, which automatically opens the occupants to 'inviting in' those negative entities that use that energy for their own entertainment.

As I entered the apartment, all four occupants were gathered in the living room. They had moved a mattress into the living room and the three girls had been sleeping on it and the young man was on the couch next to them.

One of the young women (I'll call her Wanda) said she had been physically attacked in her bedroom by an unseen force. Also, objects had been hurled across the room, loud noises had occurred throughout the apartment, and they were all totally unnerved.

I walked slowly through the apartment, following Michael's instructions... stopping when necessary. The energy was heavy and erratic. I encountered a very strong force of energy that said it was a Pagan leader of the group that had entered this home as a challenge.

When we returned to the living room, I asked if any of them had used any form of 'magic' or divination. The young man (I will call Daniel) said he was a white witch, but had been very careful in his practicing this craft.

Michael explained to them through me that the apartment complex had been built upon an ancient Pagan gathering place. When Daniel worked with his witchcraft, the group of Pagans saw this as a challenge and decided to have some fun. The Pagan 'ghosts' terrorized Daniel and his friends to the point of the attack on Wanda. The more fear in the apartment, the stronger the Pagan energy became.

Michael expelled the ghosts from the apartment and urged them not to return and told them if they did return he would forcefully re-move them as well as remove their freedom to roam. Usually we help the lost souls to their spiritual home, but this group was not willing to move away from Earth. (Remember that we have free will no matter what form we are in, whether human or spirit.)

It is extremely important to know that when you 'play' with energy, you must call on your protectors to take care of you at all times. This was an unusual case because of the cult that was awakened and also the young people involved were 'evolved' enough in their own psychic awareness that they recognized the cult's efforts to create chaos for them.

Appendix

**To Get More Information about Dale
Go to website**
www.angelspeak.net

or phone toll free 1-800-421-0505

❦

**Available for individual taped
readings in person or by phone**

❦

**Call to request a free sample copy of our
monthly newsletter:
"On Wings Of Love"
800-421-0505**

Most of the meditations on the following page have come to me from my Master Teacher, Michael, as well as contributions from my teachers Lily and Daisy, and my teacher / healer / protector, Two Feathers. Each meditation originally was created to help me to heal some portion of my own reality, but truly intended for more than myself.
As Spirit helps me to heal myself I, in turn, can help you understand how to heal yourself.

❦

**For prices,
call Dale at: 800-421-0505
(Visa, Master Card, and American Express accepted)**

Or check our website: www.angelspeak.net

Meditations Available

 The House: A wonderful journey to a beautiful house that represents your heart. Inside this house are 3 closed doors labeled Pain, Fear, & Anger. We help you to go through each of these rooms within the deep recesses of you to 'clean them up'. To help you heal the wounds from past and present.

 Meet Your Animal Guides: Journey to meet your animal guides, learn who they are and hear or feel their messages.

 Chakra Clearing: The chakra system is a part of the overall you and a major part of your health system. Let Michael guide you into the cleansing and balancing of your chakras for better health and energy.

 Astral Travel: While physical body sleeps, you often journey far distances... sometimes to visit with family or friends in spirit, sometimes it is a journey for your healing, sometimes it is just for the sake of the journey itself. Learn to do this consciously in a totally safe way.

 Healing Cell Memory: Based on Sylvia Brown's book 'Past Lives / Future Healing', this is a safe & gentle guidance into your past. Many of today's fears and illnesses can be released / healed by visiting those past lives that may be a basis for today's problems.

 Healing Body, Mind, & Soul: Discussion & meditation about control & abundance of life. Step by step guidance to working with the self with earth energy and Universal energy to cleanse and balance the total <u>you</u>.

Angelic Healing: Journey to the Angelic World to receive the energy of love and help to heal whatever wounds of life that are creating problems for you. Learn to see, hear, and feel your Angels.

Mending A Broken Heart: Relaxation and technique to release pain of a broken heart. Uses visualization to heal the energetic heart (heart chakra), as well as helping with the mental, physical, and emotional pain.

Healing Financial Stress: Guide to understanding how to remove the barriers and limitations to our ability to manifest wealth in life. Scarcity is a way of thinking as well as a way of 'being and doing'. Learn to open up to receive the abundance that is available.

Healing Grief: Death of a loved one or death of a relationship are tragic experiences. Grief, itself, is a healing tool… this meditation will help you to recreate balance in your life by working with the different stages of grief to examine and to heal the pain.

Dream Weaver: Beautiful words and music to help you get to sleep more easily. A soothing and healing journey into dream-time.

7/10/15

DISCARD

Made in the USA
Charleston, SC
23 April 2014